ADHD

A Guide to Understanding and Managing ADHD

By Louise Lowe

Table of Contents

Introduction 1

Chapter 1: What Is ADHD? 2

Chapter 2: What Causes ADHD? 12

Chapter 3: The Symptoms of ADHD 17

Chapter 4: ADHD and Its Treatments 25

Chapter 5: How to Sharpen Your Memory When You Have ADHD? 39

Chapter 6: The Do's and Don'ts of Parenting a Child with ADHD ... 48

Final Words 62

Introduction

You probably picked up this book for many reasons, but ultimately, because your life could be much smoother than it presently is. Maybe you always had to work harder in school, or you found yourself losing things you urgently need, or no matter how hard you try to get on top of daily routines, you put off tasks that seem too burdensome to complete in the moment. Despite your best intentions, life has always looked like a big ball of stress, and managing emotions has not been the easiest of tasks.

Maybe you are a parent looking for ADHD remedies for your children, or you are a spouse hoping to help your partner thrive in a world that is constantly pushing on them to do more and be more. Or perhaps, you have just discovered that ADHD runs in your family, but you don't know what this means for you or your loved ones.

Whatever inspired you to pick up this book, I hope that I will be able to offer an answer or two for all of the questions plaguing your mind, and provide guidance on how best live and thrive with ADHD.

Chapter 1: What Is ADHD?

ADHD is short for attention deficit hyperactivity disorder, a mental health condition, which is also referred to as a neurodevelopmental disorder. This condition mainly affects people's behavior and often makes the sufferer look restless, unable to concentrate, or to act impulsively. People with ADHD might come across as having above-average levels of energy and may find it hard to focus or sit still for long periods. The differences in brain development and brain activity of people with ADHD influence their attention levels and self-control. Tedious activities that require sustained attention over a long time might be difficult for people suffering from ADHD unless it is something they absolutely enjoy doing and will voluntarily engage in.

ADHD is not the result of poor parenting skills, excessive sugar consumption, or a lot of screen time, and it can be hard to explain this to non-sufferers. It is fair to say that everyone has, at some point, forgotten to turn in an assignment, misplaced their keys, or spaced out during a conversation. What sets someone with ADHD apart from someone without is how frequent these incidents are. When someone with ADHD does these things, it is very easy to assume this is normal behavior since people who do not have ADHD do them as well.

If someone with ADHD misplaces stuff all the time, shows up late for appointments, or often seems spaced out during conversations, they might come across as careless, not being time-conscious, or inattentive to those who do not have a clear understanding of ADHD and what it is.

Behavior is affected by the brain. ADHD brains develop and function much differently than neurotypical brains. If you are surrounded by the right support system, the attributes of a brain with ADHD can be extremely beneficial in certain situations; otherwise, they can be highly debilitating for the sufferer and those around them. Although AD stands for attention deficit, it does not necessarily mean people with ADHD showcase a lack of attention but rather find it difficult to regulate their attention or shift it onto the right task. Think of a brain that is jumping from one thing to the next or, the other extreme, hyper-focusing on one task. The executive function system of the brain acts like the self-management system helping to plan, prioritize and distribute efforts over different tasks. This internal system will help one inhibit their impulses and only switch from one task to the next when appropriate. These executive functions tend to develop slower in brains with ADHD.

People with ADHD tend to have a deficit in certain brain chemicals that help them function this way, like norepinephrine. This is a chemical in the body that should be a naturally occurring one. Norepinephrine, also known as NE, is a neurotransmitter that helps send signals from one nerve cell to the next. The deficiency, or lack thereof, can cause ADHD. NE usually bonds to dopamine, another chemical messenger in the body primarily responsible for feelings like pleasure, motivation, memory retention, and attention. It also helps in planning and thinking. The frontal cortex, the limbic system, the basal ganglia, and the reticular activating system all have reduced neurotransmission activity in an ADHD brain.

The limbic system is located deep inside the brain, and it helps regulate attention and emotions. The basal ganglia are found within the cerebral hemispheres and are tasked with our motor control functions, behavior, and emotions. The reticular activating system maintains consciousness, motivation, and arousals associated with behavior.

Those with ADHD tend to have an even more limited working memory than those who do not suffer from ADHD, making a simple task even more challenging, like reading the steps of a recipe and following through without referring to it multiple times. Following multistep directions can be difficult to keep up with when you have ADHD, and it is perfectly understandable to rely heavily on post-it notes; they are helpful!

Not everyone with ADHD is hyperactive. You might not see ADHD sufferers bouncing around the room, but their brains might be - you just cannot see it. This is described as internal restlessness, and it can be exhausting. Think of a mind constantly going around a hamster wheel or your brain in a ping-pong machine.

When energy is directed well, besides being beneficial, it can also be seen as creativity, curiosity, and drive. Before someone with ADHD takes advantage of their brain's strength and capabilities, they must learn to manage and control their energy. People with ADHD not only have difficulty regulating attention but also controlling their emotions, which can make them come across as too sensitive. This is often referred to as emotional dysregulation.

Both adults and children with ADHD may find it difficult to concentrate on tasks presented to them at work or school. Some confess they often find themselves daydreaming. Adult ADHD sufferers may make rushed decisions that will, in turn, adversely affect their lives. Scientifically, ADHD is the result of alterations in the brain's growth and overall development. Everybody has trouble keeping still, paying attention, or suppressing impulsive behavior from time to time. However, for some people, the issues are so prevalent and constant that they affect every part of their life: home, academic, social, and employment. ADHD is distinguished by developmental abnormalities in inattention, impulsivity, and hyperactivity. Individuals with ADHD can achieve great success in life. However, if ADHD is not identified and treated properly, it may have negative repercussions, such as lack of performance at school, family tension and disturbance, depression, marital troubles, drug abuse, delinquency, unintended accidents, and failure at work. Early diagnosis is crucial.

When symptoms of ADHD are perceived as personality defects rather than an actual mental health condition, it can harm those going through it and cause sufferers to believe that it is their fault, which affects their self-esteem and leads to other conditions, such as anxiety and depression. ADHD can be confusing for the sufferer and misleading for those around them. This can be avoided if the person suffering from ADHD, and others around them, acknowledge and understand the constant struggles one faces and, together, find strategies to help overcome these challenges. Eventually, people with ADHD stop beating themselves up about these flaws and focus on the more important things, like finding their strengths.

History of ADHD

Initially, ADHD was not referred to by this term but by a different term—hyperkinetic impulse disorder. After that, it was classified under the umbrella term of 'mental disorder' by the APA, or American Psychiatric Association, toward the latter part of the 1960s.

Here is a brief timeline of this condition that will help you better understand the history:

- In 1902, Sir George Still, a pediatrician, first mentioned ADHD and defined it as a defect in children that affected their moral control, stating that it was rather abnormal.

- Benzedrine was approved by the FDA in 1936, but in the following year, the medicine was found to display some side effects. When this medicine was given to children, their performance and behavior in school showed considerable improvement. However, these findings were largely ignored at that time.

- ADHD was not even recognized as a mental disorder in the first edition of the DSM, published in 1952. The second edition in 1968 listed hyperkinetic impulse disorder.

- By 1955, people started understanding ADHD and its nature, and the drug Ritalin was approved by the FDA, which is still used today.

- ADD finally appeared in the third edition of the DSM in place of hyperkinetic impulse disorder. In 1980, two subtypes of ADD were formed: ADD without hyperactivity and ADD with hyperactivity.

- Finally, in 1987, a revised version was published, and here, the term ADHD was used.

- The DSM was released as a fourth edition in 2000, which also identified three subtypes of ADHD, namely:

    - Predominantly inattentive type ADHD
    - Combined type ADHD

- Predominantly hyperactive-impulse type ADHD

Facts and Statistics

Before we move into greater details, here are some quick facts about ADHD that everyone should know:

- ❖ In a person's lifetime, 4.2% of women are usually diagnosed with ADHD. But the numbers are quite high in men at 13%.

- ❖ As compared to women, men are most likely to develop symptoms of ADHD. In fact, men have three times the chance of developing ADHD than women.

- ❖ There is no hard and fast rule that ADHD will happen only in childhood. People also deal with ADHD in their adulthood, and statistics show that almost 4% of adults encounter ADHD.

- ❖ On average, people are diagnosed with ADHD at the age of seven.

- ❖ Symptoms of ADHD first appear in children between three and six.

- ❖ About 6.4 million children in America have been diagnosed with this disorder. They are all between the ages of four and seventeen.

Even though the numbers differ from state to state—about 6.1 % of children in America are on ADHD medication and receiving treatment. But 23% of children with ADHD are not receiving any help.

ADD & ODD vs. ADHD

ADD

ADD is characterized by a lack of attention to detail, which results in poor organization, forgetfulness, and distractedness in work or school. Many people with ADD are unable to pay attention for long periods because they can't focus on details or stay focused on a single thing at a time. ADD is often mistaken for ADHD.

Another difference between ADD and ADHD is the age at which they are diagnosed. A person who is diagnosed with ADD before six is usually considered a young child with ADD. When a person isn't diagnosed until adulthood, the condition is often labeled as Adult Attention Deficit Disorder (AADD) or Late-Onset ADD (L-ADD). AADD and L-ADD may also be incorrectly labeled as ADHD.

ODD

A child with oppositional defiance disorder is a child who persistently shows anger, annoyance, or resentment. The DSM-5 defines ODD as an "ongoing pattern of negative behavior in children and adolescents" that includes the following characteristics:

- Often fails to control temper.

- Often fights with older people.

- Consistently ignores or refuses to follow adult demands or rules. Frequently bothers people on purpose (e.g., by starting arguments or pestering).

- Is prone to blaming others (e.g., for mistakes or misfortunes).

- Often actively does not acknowledge or deny complying with the requests of teachers (e.g., by not doing homework, by absence from class, truancy), other authority figures, and has low frustration tolerance.

Over time, children may become less engaged in fighting and more engaging in aggressive acts, such as bullying others or vandalizing property. The DSM-5 is used for diagnosing oppositional defiant disorder and borderline personality disorder. The authors of this DSM report state that the "six distinctive characteristics" are intended to set aside any concerns about whether the behavior viewed as oppositional is more extreme when the child is acting alone than when interacting with others. The reality that many of these actions appear to be more common in school-age children suggests that they may often have social salience. They may also be related to other ongoing patterns of poor social and emotional functioning.

ADHD is characterized by a persistent and chronic delay of self-regulation, which includes executive functioning. The delays in EFs cause inconsistent motivation, impulsivity, emotional deregulation, poor time management, disorganization, and procrastination. While these problems aren't explicitly stated in diagnostic criteria for ADHD, they are common.

People who suffer from ADHD, especially those who go undiagnosed, encounter a number of setbacks in life. It's easy for those who have ADHD to think everything is their fault when something goes wrong, but most of the time, they had nothing to do with it. This pessimism can affect their future with thoughts that tomorrow is going to be just as bad. Demoralizing beliefs prevent people from doing what they should because their thought patterns end up distorted.

Common ADHD Myths

Myths

- If you have one child with ADHD, all of your children will have it.
- ADHD is not a disability.
- Medication is the only treatment for ADHD.
- School teachers want active boys on medication.
- Only a psychiatrist can diagnose ADHD.
- ADHD is not a real problem or disorder. ADHD is a lack of willpower.

Facts

- Not all children in the same family have ADHD.
- ADHD is a recognized disability in the Americans with Disabilities Act (ADA) and the Individuals with Disabilities Education Act (IDEA).
- Medication is only one treatment option.
- School teachers want their students to give their best effort.

- Pediatricians, psychologists, neurologists, psychiatrists, and other mental health and medical personnel can all diagnose ADHD.

- Only medical doctors such as pediatricians, neurologists, psychiatrists, and nurse practitioners can prescribe medication.

ADHD is a neurobehavioral developmental disorder. It is a chemical abnormality in the management systems of the brain. ADHD is a formal diagnosis by major medical, psychological, and educational organizations using the Diagnostic and Statistical Manual of Mental Disorders. It is also recognized by the NIH and US Department of Education as a biologically based chemical imbalance of neurotransmitters in the brain.

Adult ADHD

Adult ADHD is a mental health condition with symptoms that can include difficulty concentrating, a lack of organization and planning skills, social interaction difficulties, and impulsivity.

People with this condition need to cope with common problems, like procrastination, social awkwardness, and long-term relationships. As a person with ADHD, the key to maintaining your overall health and wellness is to manage the symptoms. Medication and counseling can help some people, but a combination of both approaches is optimal for long-term success.

Adults who have ADHD may also be more likely to have other psychological problems, like depression and anxiety.

Chapter 2: What Causes ADHD?

No one knows precisely what causes ADHD, but research suggests that it can be inherited. ADHD is connected to physical changes in the brain, yet the environment and social factors might influence some of those changes.

Biology and Environment

Adults with ADHD may not recognize the neurological term "executive function." Still, they do know how hard it is to make plans, prioritize, organize, and stay on schedule. These executive functions all have to do with physical processes in the brain. Attention-deficit/hyperactivity disorder is connected to biology as well as heredity. Besides changes in neurotransmitter levels, brain scans have shown differences in the size of some parts of the brain in people who have ADHD. More research needs to be done, but this may explain why people occasionally develop secondary ADHD after a traumatic brain injury.

When it comes to causing ADHD, the environment while the human brain develops before and after birth matters. Oxygen deprivation, maternal substance abuse, zinc deficiency, and exposure to lead are just some of the known factors associated with attention-deficit/hyperactivity disorder. However, genetics also plays a role. For example, kids whose mothers drank alcohol before their birth are more likely to develop ADHD if they also have a dopamine-transporter susceptibility gene.

Genetics

Studies of twins have shown that siblings of a child with ADHD are much more likely to develop the condition. In addition, researchers suspect that up to 75% of the variation seen in ADHD symptoms among different individuals has to do with genetics. Why would ADHD be hereditary?

What we call ADHD today might have started as an evolutionary advantage. There are survival advantages in being restless and vigilant. Also, the impulsive curiosity we see as a behavior issue might once have kept children alive amid the uncertainties and dangers in the ancient wild.

In any event, the experts have found that several different genes appear to be involved with attention-deficit/hyperactivity disorder. These all affect chemicals called neurotransmitters that carry information between brain cells. The connections are not fully understood yet, but researchers have shown that stimulant medication is effective in ADHD patients who have the LPHN3 gene.

Social Factors

ADHD is certainly stressful, but since it is not an anxiety disorder, stress does not cause it. Instead, social factors that affect ADHD diagnosis include everything from setting boundaries of acceptable behavior to malingering.

The DSM and ICD guidelines for diagnosing ADHD are different. A British study found almost 4% of boys in the UK qualified for an ADHD diagnosis under the DSM, which is used in North America. Only 1.5% could be diagnosed under the stricter ICD criteria used in Europe. The difference can be explained by separate standards for what constitutes "normal" behavior for children in North America and Europe. This is an important difference for adults, because to be diagnosed with ADHD, they must have had the disorder in childhood.

Another social factor is substance abuse. Stimulants, one of the mainstays of ADHD treatment, are controlled substances. Secondary gain becomes an issue—who has ADHD and who is seeking drugs?

For instance, reportedly almost 10% of all US professional baseball players carry an ADHD diagnosis, compared to 2% to 5% of the general population. This occurred three years after Major League Baseball banned stimulants. Are players malingering to get performance-enhancing drugs or does hyperactivity make for better baseball players? It is impossible to know for sure.

How Does Adult ADHD Affect People?

Adult attention-deficit/hyperactivity disorder can show up in one of three different ways. Its symptoms usually center on attention problems, restlessness/impulsiveness, or a combination of the two.

Predominantly Inattentive Adult ADHD

As the name suggests, adults who have this form of attention-deficit/hyperactivity disorder have trouble focusing and are easily distracted. Their problems are much more intense than the trouble concentrating that all of us experience at one time or another. To get this ADHD diagnosis, symptoms must be much more severe, lasting for at least six months and disrupting a person's social and work life.

In detail, adults with inattention ADHD never stick to one task unless it is fun. They quickly get bored and start daydreaming, which makes them overlook details. They fail to finish most jobs. These adults will switch from one thing to another. Still, learning something new is hard for them, and being organized well enough to complete a task is almost impossible. Just like children with ADHD, these adults may not listen, or they may struggle to understand what has been said to them, and they are likely to lose the tools they need to finish a chore or assignment.

At home, someone who is suffering from adult inattentive ADHD may appear to not be listening. That person probably is listening but may simply be confused because they process information more slowly.

Predominantly Hyperactive/Impulsive ADHD

When children have this form of attention-deficit/hyperactivity disorder, they cannot sit still. By the time they reach adulthood, these ADHD patients will have learned ways to handle the jitters, although they are still impulsive.

Adults with hyperactive/impulsive ADHD are restless and get frustrated or angry easily. They dislike sitting around and prefer tasks that are both physically and emotionally demanding. You are more likely to meet them in work that is not sedentary and that requires constant activity. If their regular duties are not stimulating enough, these adults with ADHD will work longer hours or take on another job, not because they have to for financial reasons but because they strive to keep busy.

Socializing with someone who has the hyperactive/impulsive form of adult ADHD can be a little like crossing a minefield. Such people are often intense, and it does not take much to irritate them. Besides being prone to lose their temper, they may easily become frustrated and impatient. Their impulsivity leads to reckless behavior as well as snap decisions that often do not work out well for anyone.

Diagnosing Adult ADHD

Adult attention-deficit/hyperactivity disorder may also show up as a combination of the two types described above in detail. Regardless of type, ADHD disrupts family and social ties in ways that are difficult for others to understand. Since ADHD is often considered a childhood disease, adults with the disorder often go untreated. This situation is slowly changing.

No sure-fire test can instantly diagnose adult ADHD. Healthcare professionals must look carefully at adult and childhood symptoms, as told to them not only by the patient but also by family members, friends, teachers, and others who knew the patient as a child. Then, the healthcare providers have to rule out possible physical problems as well as other mental health issues that might cause the symptoms in question.

It does not help that adults, particularly those with high intelligence, tend to compensate for the symptoms. They may do this so effectively that they completely avoid seeking help.

Chapter 3: The Symptoms of ADHD

Children's Symptoms

Make Irresponsible Mistakes

Kids with ADHD have issues filtering or regulating themselves socially, mentally, and physically. Compare the frontal part of the brain—where the ADHD physically resides—to a coffee filter whose job is to regulate or control what goes into the coffee pot. The filter allows water to go through but not the grounds. The filter of an ADHD child isn't working as well as it should, which means their mind will have more difficulty regulating what comes out through their behavior and emotions.

Let's look at a situation where an ADHD boy is being teased. Multiple ideas pop into his mind about how to react and handle this situation, and because the filter is not properly functioning as it should, he may respond inappropriately, such as pushing or hitting another child.

Fidgeting

They fidget. Some kids with ADHD fidget a lot. They may move their arms and legs, rub their eyes, or tap their pencil on the table.

Temper Tantrums

They have temper tantrums. These can make a child hard to live with. The tantrums usually occur when the kids are overtired, hungry, or upset for some other reason. When they do not attain what they desire, they show it by acting out.

Egocentric

Most children with ADHD are self-centered. They have a difficult time seeing and understanding other people's feelings. Because of their poor impulse control and short attention span, they sometimes come across as aloof or self-centered.

Uncompleted Tasks

Children with ADHD have a difficult time finishing their work. They are easily distracted and lose interest in an activity before it's finished, even if they are interested initially.

Absence of Concentration

Children with ADHD have trouble paying attention. Kids with ADHD struggle to stay focused on one thing. This makes it difficult for them to learn how to read or write, do math, or participate in games at the same speed as their classmates. They often get bored quickly and need to switch activities often.

Playing Quietly Isn't an Option.

ADHD kids also tend to be hyper-talkers. They may have problems regulating how much and how fast they talk with seemingly no regard for interrupting others. And because their internal thoughts often travel faster than they can talk, what they say may only be part of their point, causing confused communication.

Having Issues Waiting

They can also be irritable because their impulses make it hard to understand social rules.

Avoidance

They tend to avoid responsibility. They don't want to do things that are hard, boring, or unpleasant. They prefer to follow their own ideas and have a hard time following directions and doing things they don't want to do.

Not Well-Organized

This makes it a problem for them to get their work done on time, help their friends, and follow through on tasks.

Daydreaming

They like to daydream. They have trouble staying focused on what's going on around them. They may easily space out and lose track of time.

Adults' Symptoms

Mood Swings

Emotions play an integral role in all our mental processes, our impulses, and our decision-making. Since ADHD can make our highs and lows seem extreme, many of our thought processes and decisions can seem extreme, as well. Because the intensity of these emotions can make us fixate on them to the exclusion of anything else, we can feel like our brain has been completely taken over by something that most people would see as a minor issue. When we are pumped about something, we go all in.

When we get rejected, it can feel like the apocalypse. When we are frustrated, we can get so overwhelmed by negativity that we just shut down. Things can feel so intensely challenging that it is easy to get completely discouraged. However, these intense emotional reactions to difficult situations don't have to lead to self-destructive actions. Frustrations can be a powerful driving force for creativity.

Hyperfocus

This is probably one of the less frequently mentioned ADHD traits, and it is connected to your brain's hunger for dopamine. Dopamine is sort of like a doggy biscuit for your brain. If you teach your puppy to shake hands and roll over three times, all while howling the happy birthday song, and then you give him a treat, he will keep on doing it over and over because he wants the treat.

When we find something that triggers a dopamine reward in the brain, we want to keep it going for as long as possible.

This mechanism may be what gives us the unique ability to focus on an enjoyable activity without stopping, possibly for hours on end. For many of us, it is video games. For others, it may be working on a complicated art project. You probably already understand that there are some things you can do for hours. Of course, the downside to your ability to focus exclusively on one enjoyable activity is that all the other things that should be on your to-do list fade behind the backdrop of your intense engagement. Your brain kicks into overdrive and produces that enjoyable rush that keeps you plugged into your task.

If you were (or still are) one of those kids that would play video games for six hours straight, not even pausing to eat, drink, or go to the bathroom, you are probably familiar with this sensation. Everything else disappears. It is just you versus the zombies for hours and hours. Any interruption that breaks the positive feedback loop is an unwelcome and painful experience. When you stop, the world comes flooding back in. You realize that you are hungry, thirsty, it's super late, you haven't even started your homework, and you really need to go to the bathroom.

The ADHD brain kicks into high gear when it is highly interested in something. This hyperfocus would have been, and still is for some, essential for hunters on the chase or fighters engaged in combat on the war front.

We have been told that people with ADHD can't pay attention for long periods of time, but that's not even remotely true. They are actually capable of paying attention more intensely than a lot of people, but only if it is on something they find interesting that rewards them with extra dopamine.

Forgetful

Adults who have ADHD tend to forget things, especially when they are tired. They will not be able to accomplish tasks unless they have enough rest or sleep.

Problems with Time Management

If you find it hard to prioritize tasks and keep track of how much time you have left before a deadline, you may have Adult ADHD.

Disorganization

If you find it hard to organize your life and plan ahead, you may have Adult ADHD. You will also find that when it comes to completing tasks, you tend to scope out the work required before doing anything.

Having Trouble Focusing

If you are easily distracted, forgetful, or have problems focusing on the task at hand for long periods of time, you might be suffering from Adult ADHD.

Impulsiveness

Impulsivity is what allows us to make snap decisions. In a fast-paced, high-risk environment, this is an advantage. It would give us the ability to do things, like jumping from a runaway horse before it gallops straight into a ravine. This same impulsiveness would have allowed the deer hunter to drop everything and suddenly veer off course in favor of following bear tracks. In a less intense environment, this is not always an advantage. Sometimes, we do things without thinking about the consequences. Whether your impulses tell to see how fast you can get your car up to a hundred miles per hour, or to go cliff diving in the quarry by yourself at night during a thunderstorm, this trait can result in consequences that range from mildly embarrassing to devastating. I'm sure you may already have some experience with this.

But this impulsivity might also be described as spontaneity or flexibility. Yes, you might do things that logic cannot possibly explain, but this ability to quickly change course or to pursue a sudden opportunity without overthinking it can lead to some fantastic results!

Hypercritical

Adults who suffer from ADHD have trouble controlling their anger and impulses, which will often cause them to lash out at people around them.

Nervousness

Adults who have ADHD will often suffer from anxiety, and they may find it difficult to relax. They will also find that the smallest problems stress them out and leave them feeling on edge.

Lack of Motivation

Waiting until the last minute to work on a task is classic ADHD. We will put things off for as long as humanly possible, typically making things into an emergency situation before we realize that there is no way to put off that project, paper, or presentation any longer. For example, let's say you get a parking ticket but put off paying it for weeks and weeks. You just aren't motivated to shell out that twenty dollars until you find out that they won't let you register for your next semester's classes if you don't pay up. So, now that the last day for course registration is upon you and the situation is urgent, you get the ticket paid and finally get to sign up for your courses. This experience is all too familiar.

Obviously, one of the problems with this is that sometimes we wait too long, then we can't quite pull things off the way we had hoped. But I'm sure that you also know the flip side. Once you've created a crisis of epic proportions, adrenaline kicks in, and your brain finally gets the stimulation it was striving for. This lets you channel your energy and focus on getting your work done.

Exhaustion

Adults who have ADHD tend to feel tired all the time, and obviously your symptoms only worsen when you don't get enough sleep. You may also experience poor performance at work or school. If you feel like your work or school performance is slipping because you can't sleep, this could be a sign of Adult ADHD.

Chapter 4: ADHD and Its Treatments

If you are looking out for ways to improve the symptoms of ADHD that are affecting either you or a loved one, you will have to seek treatment. You will likely be given the options of medication or therapy. However, to get the best results, maintaining a proper balance of the two is always suggested.

Medication

To treat ADHD, there are a total of five types of medicines that can be used. However, before we can move forward with discussing these medications, you will have to keep in mind that you will never get a permanent cure for ADHD. So, it can be said that even if you opt for medication, your child will get only some temporary relief from the symptoms. They will regain the capability to practice new skills, have a calmer demeanor, and focus for a period of time. Some medications can only be administered in intervals, while others can be given to your child on a regular basis. As always, make sure you are only taking medications prescribed to you by a medical professional, and be sure to consult with them if you are experiencing side effects or if the medication isn't providing the desired results. Not all ADHD treatments will work equally for everyone, and a bit of trial and error is often required to find the right treatment and dosage.

Regardless of the medication type that is administered to a child, they will never be provided with large starting doses for safety's sake. To properly administer the effects of the medications on your child and also to get him/her used to them, small doses will be suggested. With passing time, the doses can be either be decreased or increased gradually if something of this sort is necessary. Also, you will have to take your child for regular checkups to the concerned specialist for regular monitoring. The specialist will also tell you after some time whether the prescribed medications or dosage are actually helping your child or not. If you find that your child experiences side effects from the medications, never hesitate to tell the specialist. Some of the common medications that are used for ADHD treatment are:

- **Dexamphetamine:** This medication can be provided to any person who is above five years old. It is consumed as a tablet. In some cases, this medication might be prescribed two times a day. In general, it is administered once every day. However, dexamphetamine might also result in side effects, such as a reduction in appetite, mood swings, dizziness, and headaches, among various others.

- **Methylphenidate:** You can regard this medication as the most common and most widely used one for treating ADHD. The primary reason behind the popularity of this medication is that it can be provided to anyone over five years old. Some of the common side effects of this medication include increased blood pressure and heart rate, stomach aches, and lack of sleep.

- **Guanfacine:** This medication reduces blood pressure and also helps in improving attentive power. It is meant for kids around five. The medication is not meant for adults.

Therapy

Another option that you can choose is therapy. You can select from various types of therapies. Let us have a look at them:

- **Psychoeducation:** Therapy of this sort helps in making it easier to diagnose and also understand ADHD symptoms. During these sessions, you and your child will have to speak up about ADHD and identify which of its symptoms you experience.

- **Behavior Therapy:** In this type of therapy, not only is the child with ADHD involved, but also their parents and teachers. A proper system is developed in which the child will get some kind of reward for showing good behavior, which means desired behaviors can easily be instilled with this method.

- **Social Skills Training:** In this type of therapy, the concept of role-playing is put into use to help the child learn how to socialize with others. They also come to know about certain behaviors that they should opt for when in a public setting.

- **Parent Training:** Programs of this type are meant specifically for the parents in order to make them aware of some new techniques with which they can easily improve the symptoms of their child. Mostly group programs are used for this where parents can discuss with the parents of other children about their shared experiences.

Mindfulness

ADHD can show up at different stages of life and in several ways. It occurs due to differences in the brain, which affect important functioning skills, like memory, attention, impulsiveness, concentration, and more. For a majority of children and adults suffering from ADHD, maintaining self-regulation and paying attention are two of the persistent daily challenges that they have to face. So, a natural remedy for ADHD would be some kind of attention training that helps hone their self-control.

While the symptoms of ADHD can be managed by therapy and medication, they are not the only options. According to studies, another good way to improve your focus and calm your mind is through mindful meditation. Mindfulness or mindful meditation is a part of several religious traditions, like Buddhism. However, it is not necessarily spiritual or religious. It consists of developing a greater awareness of everything that is happening around you by paying close attention to your bodily sensations, feelings, and thoughts. It can also be used as a tool to promote psychological well-being.

Is Mindfulness Effective for ADHD?

Just like exercises can help strengthen a specific weak muscle in your body, the same thing can also be true for your brain. Mindfulness helps enhance your capacity to control your attention. It allows you to focus on yourself and teaches you how to observe yourself. In addition to that, when you get distracted, mindfulness trains you to bring back your wandering mind to the present moment.

Unlike other treatments for ADHD, practicing mindfulness helps to develop your inner skills. It helps increase your ability to develop different kinds of relationships, to train your attention, and to strengthen your ability to self-observe so that you can control your attention.

Meditation thickens the prefrontal cortex of your brain. The prefrontal cortex is the region of your brain that is involved in controlling your impulses, planning, and focusing. It also increases the level of dopamine in your brain, which gets decreased in people who have ADHD.

If you find long durations of sitting meditation to be overwhelming, here are a few ways to help you get started:

- ❖ **Take a Class.** You can try signing up for a meditation class to harness the power of positive peer pressure. Following routines can be hard for people suffering from ADHD, so it is hard for them to practice sitting down for a long period of time. Having a structure and group support can be helpful for them so that they don't feel like they are doing it alone.

   Some centers provide eight-week programs that have weekly training sessions of two-and-a-half hours each, along with an at-home practice. They generally begin with seated meditations for five minutes every day at home then work up to fifteen to twenty minutes. They may also provide you with the option of practicing longer or replacing seated meditation with mindful walking.

   However, your ADHD won't get much better if you do it for just a few minutes a day. Even though the meditation sessions are essential, the key is to be mindful of your actions throughout the day by being aware of where you are focused while you're performing your daily activities. For instance, you might notice that when you are behind the wheel, your attention often goes to the chores you need to do later that day. A majority of people follow mindfulness while eating. You can use the techniques of mindfulness anytime you begin to feel overwhelmed once you are accustomed to checking in with your mind and body.

- ❖ **Make It Your Own.** Individuals with ADHD are encouraged to use mindfulness while performing their daily activities. You can even practice mindfulness on your own. Simply, choose a comfortable place where no one will disturb you, sit down, and spend five minutes concentrating on the feelings of breathing in and breathing out. Concentrate on how you feel when your stomach rises and falls. In some time, you will begin to notice that your mind is wandering off to something else—your plans for the day or some noise you just heard or your job. Label these thoughts as "thinking" and put your attention back on your breath. Try to perform this mental exercise every day. Increase the duration of time you spend on the mental training every couple of weeks—ten minutes, fifteen, up to twenty minutes, or even more if you want to. Try performing the same exercise every day and concentrate on your breath for some time as you are sitting in front of your computer, or when you are stopped at a red light, or when you are walking from one place to another. By doing this, you can eventually practice mindfulness at any moment, even while you are conversing with others. Turning on your state of mind-awareness at any time during the day is a great exercise, even if it is only for a few minutes. You are essentially letting go of the busyness of your thoughts and bringing your focus back to everything that is happening in the present moment in daily life.

- ❖ **Practice Self-Compassion.** People suffering from the challenges of ADHD for several years can be left with crippled self-esteem. You can learn to be more accepting of your weaknesses and strengths through self-compassion. Having an attitude of acceptance can also help improve and manage your areas of weaknesses. For instance, if you are more compassionate toward your problems with time management, you don't have to pretend that you don't have a problem. You can get proactive about having the tools to manage your time properly without having to feel shameful every time you are late.

Studies examining the non-pharmacological interventions for individuals suffering from ADHD have increased in recent years and have provided several more treatment options for patients. Current empirical studies support the logic behind using mindfulness techniques to alleviate ADHD symptoms. In one study, a mindful meditation program conducted in a group was administered to a sample of adolescents and adults with ADHD for eight weeks. Pre- and post-treatment assessments showed that there was an improvement in anxious, depressive, hyperactive-impulsive, and inattentive symptoms.

A study conducted in 2008 with eight adolescents and twenty-five adults, half of whom suffered from the combined type of ADHD (both hyperactive and inactive), revealed promising results. Significant improvements in both hyperactivity and inattention were observed through the study. The cognitive tests showed that the participants improved their ability to stay focused on one thing even when several other things were competing for their attention. It was also revealed that the majority of them felt less sad and stressed out when the study was completed.

The *Journal of Child and Family Studies* released a study in 2011 over the outcome of a mindfulness-based training program that took place over eight weeks. The participants included children between eight and twelve, and parallel mindful training was also being conducted for their parents. The study reported a significant decrease in the symptoms of ADHD, as were reported by the parents after the eight-week training program. There was also a decrease in over-reactivity and parental stress.

Exercise

Just like mindful meditation, exercise is another method of treatment for ADHD that doesn't require a visit to a therapist's office or a prescription. Studies show that exercising regularly can improve the symptoms of ADHD in adults and also improve their thinking ability.

Studies have shown that exercise is not only good for toning muscles and shedding fat; it can also help you to keep your brain in good shape. Broad science says that exercise can help manage ADHD by increasing the release of neurotransmitters like norepinephrine and dopamine, which help with clear thinking and attention. Individuals suffering from ADHD tend to have a lesser amount of dopamine in their brains. The stimulants and medicines that are used for the treatment of ADHD in adults increase the level of dopamine available to the brain. Regular exercise can raise the baseline levels of norepinephrine and dopamine by increasing the development of several new receptors in specific regions of the brain.

Exercise also helps to balance the level of norepinephrine in the arousal center located in the stem of the brain. The abilities of the locus coeruleus are improved through regular exercise. As a result, people are less prone to react out of proportion or get startled because of any given situation. They also feel less irritable. In the same way, exercise also administers the transmission fluids for the basal ganglia, which causes smooth changes in the attention system. This region is an essential site for binding stimulants, and brain scans also reveal that it is not normal in people suffering from ADHD.

Exercising can benefit other regions of the brain as well. For example, an overactive cerebellum can contribute to fidgetiness. According to several recent studies, these regions are brought back into balance by ADHD medications that increase the levels of norepinephrine and dopamine.

Some of the benefits that exercise can provide for adults suffering from ADHD are:

- ❖ Improved levels of brain-derived neurotrophic factors that are involved in memory and learning.

This protein is present in lesser amounts in people suffering from ADHD.

- ❖ Improved executive functions that are required to remember details, organize, and plan.

- ❖ Improved working memory.

- ❖ Decreased compulsive behavior and improved impulse control.

- ❖ Eased anxiety and stress.

Any kind of physical activities, like skateboarding, whitewater rafting, mountain biking, rock climbing, gymnastics, ice skating, ballet, and martial arts, are good for adults suffering from ADHD. The technical movements used to perform these kinds of physical activities trigger an array of brain regions that help control intense focus and concentration, inhibition, fine motor adjustments, error connection, switching, evaluating consequences, sequencing, timing, and control balance. In the extreme, engaging in these activities also becomes a matter of survival—preventing yourself from drowning in the swirling pool of whitewater, or hurting yourself on the balance beam, or avoiding a punch. Thus, it helps you tap into the concentrating power of your mind's fight-or-flight response. You feel plenty of motivation to learn the techniques that are required for such activities when your mind is on high alert. For the brain, it would feel like a do-or-die situation.

Exercise also helps regulate the amygdala and has a positive effect on the limbic system. In people with ADHD, the amygdala can help blunt the hair-trigger responsiveness that is experienced by many. This prevents you from going overboard and creating a scene out of anger.

Common Types of Exercises that Help Alleviate the Symptoms of ADHD

For a majority of patients, exercise is recommended as a method to help manage their symptoms. Several studies have revealed that one of the best treatments for children and adults with ADHD is regular exercise. This is mainly because exercise helps them get rid of the extra raw energy present in a healthy manner. Here are some of the common types of exercises that help alleviate the symptoms of ADHD:

- **Walking.** Walking is one of the simplest aerobic exercises that you can do. What's great about walking is that it can be done by almost anyone of any age group. All you require is a comfy pair of shoes. Walking helps tone your leg muscles and also increases your heart rate. Children and adults suffering from ADHD can also benefit from being outside surrounded by nature. Research conducted on children with ADHD revealed that walking in the park for twenty minutes can help improve their concentration.

- **Dancing.** Many people suffering from ADHD find dance classes appealing as a social form of exercise. The best kinds of dances are those involving fast-paced movements that give you the opportunity to release all your extra energy. Research conducted in Sweden with boys aged five to seven found that participating in dance classes helped them increase their concentration while doing their schoolwork and also helped to calm them down.

- **Swimming.** Swimming is another aerobic exercise that can help you tone your muscles and improve your cardiovascular health. People suffering from ADHD can get a boost from being on a swim team because they have to perform individually even though they are on a team. It might be hard for people suffering from ADHD to be a part of a sports team if they have to spend a lot of time just waiting for their turn to play. An individual sport like swimming can be a great exercise for this reason.

- **Yoga.** Yoga is deliberate and slow, while people suffering from ADHD are hyperactive. Research has revealed that yoga can be a good form of exercise for you, even if you are suffering from ADHD because it helps you to focus on yourself. It teaches you to pay attention to your own body and concentrate on your breathing. It forces you to be in the present moment by becoming grounded. Doing yoga can, thus, help you learn how to concentrate and focus better.

- **Martial Arts.** Different forms of martial arts, like tai chi, aikido, tae-kwon-do, and karate, etc., require your full attention both mentally and physically. In addition to that, martial arts have a set of fixed rules that need to be followed. This helps add more structure to your everyday life. They can help you feel relaxed and focused, at the same time, and this can help you alleviate your symptoms of ADHD. One of the most helpful martial arts is tai chi, as it is also a meditative practice. It can help boost your concentration skills and relieve your stress. Research has revealed that practicing tai chi regularly can help you develop higher levels of self-confidence and focus during other activities. You get trained in several skills, like fine motor skills, consequences of actions, memory, timing, balance, focus, and concentration when you practice martial arts.

- **Strength Training.** You can add in some strength work, like weightlifting, pull-ups, pushups, squats, and lunges in order to build more muscle and burn off excess energy.

Similar to medication, exercise can also help you alleviate the symptoms of ADHD if you continue using it on a regular basis. Here are some tips to help you stay on course if you have difficulty sticking to an exercise program:

- **Move in the Morning.** Try exercising first thing in the morning if it fits in your schedule. Doing it in the morning before you have taken your medications can help you get the most benefits from the medications that you are going to take throughout the day to boost your mood. It can also help set the right tone for the rest of the day.

- **Find a Partner.** Exercising with a workout buddy can help pass the time and help you stay on track while you sweat.

- **Keep It Interesting.** Mix different types of exercises in your routine. If you change your activity every week or every day, it can help you stay out of a rut.

Just like any medications, the effects of exercise can only last for a specific time. Consider your workout routine as a dose of treatment. Try to exercise for thirty to forty minutes at least once a day, four to five days a week. It is up to you to choose the kind of exercise you want to do, but make sure that it is moderately intense so that your muscles feel tired, you sweat, you breathe harder and faster, and your heart rate goes up during the workout session. If you are not sure about how intense your routine should be, you should always consult your doctor.

Chapter 5: How to Sharpen Your Memory When You Have ADHD?

People with ADHD often suffer from executive function (EF) deficits. Some of the most profound impairments are linked with working memory, fluid intelligence, processing speed, planning, vigilance, and response inhibition. These EF deficits can be seen as a sign of lower intelligence and can lead to reduced self-esteem, decreased professional or academic achievements, and reduced income. It is thought that the intelligence deficits seen in people who have ADHD are caused because of impairments in higher-order cognitive processes, like working memory, and not due to direct impairment of cognitive abilities.

A majority of people who have ADHD have problems with working memory. Occasionally, most of us will forget important dates or lose our keys. You might think that these things happen because you are inattentive. However, when these turn into habits, you might have a poor working memory associated with ADHD. People with ADHD might have problems differentiating between important and unimportant cues, organizing, focusing, and recalling things. It might be hard for them to get started on tasks, and they might become forgetful or get distracted easily. It is often impossible and frustrating for them to follow lengthy multi-step directions. Sharpening their working memory can help strengthen a person's problem-solving skills, control impulsive behaviors, and improve their ability to focus.

What Is Working Memory?

The terms *working memory* and *short-term memory* are often used interchangeably. You might have heard either of these terms before. The terms refer to a "temporary storage system" that is located in the brain to store various thoughts and facts while you are performing a task or solving a problem. Thus, it allows you to store information and thoughts temporarily in your mind so that you can use them whenever you need them to finish a task. Working memory helps you to hold facts and thoughts for long enough so that you can use it in a short while, remember what to do next, and concentrate on your task at hand.

You can consider working memory to be a shelf in your brain. For example, you have to go to the supermarket because you need bread, eggs, and milk. While you are shopping for these things in the supermarket, you suddenly remember that you have to buy cereal as well. So, you go to the cereal aisle. However, having to buy eggs falls off your mental shelf as you focus on buying the cereal. You come back home with bread, milk, and cereal and realize that you have forgotten to buy the eggs.

The total number of things that you can accommodate on your mental shelf might be different than the number that another person can store in his working memory. Studies have revealed that young children can hold only one or two things in their working memory as they have limited working memory skills. It continues to develop until one reaches fifteen. However, not everyone has the same capacity for working memory, and it doesn't develop at the same pace for everyone. Some people can accommodate more items in their mental shelf than others.

Scientists don't agree on the number of information "bytes" that the brain can hold. According to some, it's around four, while others claim that it's as many as seven items. Several studies have also been conducted, which showed that one's working memory could be strengthened and improved. You can increase your capacity for working memory by grouping things together. For instance, a phone number generally consists of ten digits; however, we often divide the number into three separate groups. It helps us to remember the ten-digit number by making use of only three working memory slots. Working memory is similar to plastic—trainable, movable, and flexible. It is just like our muscles and can be improved with the help of training and exercise.

When Do We Use Working Memory?

Working memory is used in various situations. We use it to follow multi-step directions, do mental math, follow a conversation, organize, plan, write, or read. It helps us to stay engaged and focused on a task. Working memory is also important for students. Recent research conducted in the United Kingdom with around 3,000 junior high and grade-school students revealed that struggles in school were caused mostly due to weak working memory and not because of low IQ. Studies also showed that almost all of the students who had a poor working memory scored less in math and reading comprehension.

Here are some examples of how your daily life is affected by weak working memory:

- ❖ Your inability to follow through on projects and your disorganization causes you to miss deadlines at work.

- ❖ In order to retain information, you have to reread something multiple times.

- ❖ You plan to work from the comfort of your house; however, you don't remember to bring the required items with you.

- ❖ You get distracted from work and have several unfinished projects.

- ❖ While having a conversation with someone, you forget what the other person has just said and have difficulty following a conversation.

- ❖ Even when you were just told the directions to a place, you tend to get lost easily.

- ❖ You keep losing your wallet, cell phone, or keys.

- ❖ You wish to participate in a conversation. However, you forget what you wanted to say by the time the other person has finished speaking.

You require the help of your working memory no matter what you want to do.

You can use a number of services and products (for example, Play Attention and CogMed) to strengthen your working memory and train your brain. Several studies have revealed that such products and services can improve your working memory; however, the benefits might not last beyond the training session. Other studies have, however, shown that if you commit to training your brain, it can significantly improve your working memory.

The first step to strengthening your working memory is by understanding your own limitations and knowing how memory works. People who have ADHD often try to keep things in order by using reminder systems. They might keep a list of things they need to buy at the grocery store or keep a running to-do list on a notepad app on their tablet or phone. They might also use a calendar app or a timer to remind them of their appointments.

Tips to Boost Working Memory

Here are some tips on how you can improve your working memory:

- ❖ **Include Exercise in Your Daily Routine.** According to a few studies, exercising regularly can improve your working memory. Researchers believe that physical activity and exercise can improve the health of brain cells. It can also reduce stress, help you sleep better, and improve your mood—all of which can indirectly influence your memory and affect your cognitive abilities.

- ❖ **Using Mindfulness to Strengthen Your Working Memory and Reduce Distractions.** Research conducted by MIT, Massachusetts General Hospital, and Harvard Medical School found that practicing mindfulness techniques daily can improve recall and also allowed the participants to regulate their sensory output and tune out any distractions.

- ❖ **Decrease Multitasking.** A study conducted at the University of Sussex found that multitasking can decrease activity in particular regions of your brain and is also associated with a reduced attention span. Try finishing the task at hand before moving on to the next task.

- **Try Different Methods of Remembering Information.** Making up a rhyme or creating a song might make it easier for you to remember a list of things. Some might also find it easier to remember multiple things by visualizing them. Visualize yourself stopping at the grocery store when you are coming home from work and picking up yogurt, bread, cheese, and milk. Try to imagine what it would look like to go to each section of the store. You are more likely to remember all the items you need to purchase at the grocery store if you follow your visualization because images and visuals can be more powerful than words.

- **Develop Routines.** When you return from work, start by creating a routine. As soon as you walk through your door, choose a specific place to keep your keys and cell phone. Keep them in the same place every time when you return from work.

- **Use Checklists for Tasks that Have Several Steps.** Try making a checklist for your first hour at work. It could include several tasks, like reviewing yesterday's progress, checking and replying to emails, returning calls, listening to messages, checking with the supervisor for the necessary tasks that need to be finished immediately, etc.

- ❖ **Divide Large Chunks of Information into Smaller Pieces.** Before moving forward to the next instruction, concentrate on one or two of them first. For instance, if you want to get ready to host a party in your house but are stressed and overwhelmed about everything that you need to get done, like setting up, cleaning the house, cooking, and shopping, try concentrating on a single area at one time, like shopping. Forget about the remaining tasks until you have finished shopping.

- ❖ **Practice Your Skills of Working Memory.** You can create your own brain training programs or use the ones mentioned above. Jot down six words that are unrelated to each other. Begin by trying to remember the first two words without seeing the paper. Then, as you succeed, add another word to the sequence.

Working memory is used by children all the time to learn things. They need it for solving math problems in their heads or following multi-step directions. You can help your child strengthen their working memory by incorporating some simple strategies into their daily lives. Here are some tips by which you can boost your child's working memory:

- ❖ **Help Make Connections.** Help your kid create links that associate various details and make them memorable. Using fun mnemonics is another great way to grab your kid's attention. Finding ways to link different information also helps in creating and recovering long-term memories. It can also help with working memory with which they can hold and compare recent and old memories.

- ❖ **Make It Multisensory.** Processing information using multiple senses can help improve long-term memory as well as working memory. Jot down certain tasks for your kid so that they can look at them. Let your child hear them when you say them out loud. Walk with your kid through your house while telling them about the family chores that they need to finish. When you use multisensory strategies, it helps your kids store the information in their minds for long enough to use it.

- ❖ **Encourage Active Reading.** Highlighting or underlining text and jotting down notes can help children keep the facts in their minds for long enough to answer questions about them. This is why sticky notes and highlighters are so popular nowadays. Asking questions about the text and reading it out loud can also help with their working memory. Long-term memories can also be formed with the help of these active reading strategies.

- ❖ **Play Cards.** Easy card games, like War, Go Fish, Uno, and Crazy Eights, can help strengthen your kid's working memory in two ways. Not only do they have to remember and maintain the rules of the game they are playing, but they also need to keep in mind the cards they have and the ones the other players have played.

- ❖ **Play Games that Use Visual Memory.** Kids can improve their visual memory by playing matching games. You can also try giving your child a page from a magazine and tell them to mark all the instances of the letter "a" or the word "the." It may also be fun to use license plates and recite the numbers and letters on them and taking turns to recite them backward as well.

- ❖ **Have Your Children Teach You.** When you can explain how to perform or do something to others, it involves understanding the information and filing it mentally. For instance, if your kid is learning how to dribble a basketball, ask them to teach you how to do it. Teachers also do something similar to this when they pair up students in a class. Doing this allows them to work with the facts instantly instead of waiting to be called on.

Chapter 6: The Do's and Don'ts of Parenting a Child with ADHD

A child with ADHD likely often loses track of things, finds it difficult to stay on top of homework, and appears to be generally unfocused when attending to tasks or chores. These symptoms can present parents with several challenges on a day-to-day basis. Raising a child with ADHD is no easy feat. It's also worth mentioning that there are no hard and fast rules since this disorder can vary in terms of symptoms and their severity. With that said, children with ADHD can tremendously benefit from customized person-centered approaches. ADHD can cause children to lack impulse control, leading to poor and often inappropriate behavior. It is this impulsivity that pushes your child to be defiant and to argue.

Their tendency to get overstimulated results in them overreacting to frustration and failure. So as a parent, you must understand and recognize ADHD as a functional difference in your child's brain. This doesn't mean that your child is unable to learn the distinction between right and wrong - it simply means you need to find other ways to support them in cultivating positive behavior. The tendency to get distracted, the penchant for hyperactivity, and the inclination to be impulsive are at the root of all misbehavior. These three elements often make it harder for your child to develop the necessary skills and assimilate the tools they need to control their attention, emotions, behavior, and activity. For instance, your child may not seem to listen, and they may have trouble following directions or putting in the needed effort to succeed in their schoolwork. They may be disorganized, messy, and impatient. They may do things they shouldn't without giving them a second thought. They may interrupt conversations and express an unwillingness to wait, take turns, or share. They may even lose their temper, throw tantrums, and have emotional outbursts.

When you lose perspective, you don't realize that these symptoms are all the product of ADHD, which often makes you feel stressed, frustrated, and inadequate as a parent. You may even feel embarrassed when your child misbehaves in public to the point where you think you're the reason they turned out the way they did, but you have to understand that the skills and tools typical children use that help them regulate their attention, activity, and behavior simply don't come as naturally to children with ADHD. As a parent, you can only learn about your child's disorder, figure out the parenting approaches that work best, and help your child improve and succeed. This process can be long, strenuous, and challenging at times, but you have to remember that you are an adult, and it's up to you to respond in a way that makes your child's ADHD better, not worse. Consistency is of vital importance for your child, so you may need to adjust your ways of interacting with them, whether it be your speech, gestures, emotional language, or the physical environment itself.

When you begin to implement a supportive and structured methodology in your parenting, you will see that difficult behavior can be limited, allowing your child to thrive and flourish. In this section, we will delve into the dos and don'ts of parenting kids with ADHD.

The Do's

This compilation of tips will help you deal with the challenges of this disorder to ultimately reduce disruptive behavior in your child.

Be Involved

Being involved is an essential step in helping your child manage their ADHD. So, make sure you follow the treatment your child's therapist has recommended, keep track of all therapy appointments, and if your child has been prescribed medicine, give it to them at the time suggested by their provider. Do not alter the dosage or compensate for it if you miss a day; always check with your doctor first. You also need to ensure that the medicine is stored in a safe place that only you and your partner have access to.

Understand How ADHD Affects Your Child

Not every child with ADHD is the same, they won't necessarily share the same struggles in their day-to-day lives. Some kids may have more trouble paying attention while others may find it more difficult to settle down. So, you need to build awareness and cultivate a better understanding of how ADHD affects your child in particular. Asking your child's therapist for tips you can use to help your child improve can go a long way.

Determine Which Behaviors Are Acceptable and Which Are Not Ahead of Time

The entire premise of behavioral modification revolves around teaching your child to consider the consequences of their actions to engender better control of the impulses they have. This process requires a lot of patience, empathy, affection, and strength on the part of the parents. So, you have to decide ahead of time which behaviors are acceptable and which behaviors you won't tolerate. Sticking to the guidelines you establish is as important as determining those guidelines in the first place.

Punishing your child one day for a pattern of behavior then allowing it to happen the next not only confuses your child but impedes their improvement over time. Admittedly, some behaviors should always be deemed unacceptable, for instance, refusing to turn off the TV or to get up in the morning when you tell them to do so. Because your child may have a hard time grasping these guidelines, you need to make them as simple and as clear as possible.

Set Structure But Make It Pressure-Free

Structure is of the utmost importance when raising a child with ADHD. If they have no sense of routine, you cannot expect them to be disciplined and follow the rules when their habits are all out of place. Introducing structure to your household may involve setting charts to help your child understand what they need to do, putting up planners and calendars to help them visualize time, and determining clear rules and sensible routines to govern their daily life, especially at bedtime or right after they wake up in the morning. When you make it easier for your child to follow the structure you fixed, this can greatly reduce their distractibility and disorganized tendencies.

Define the Rules But Allow a Degree of Flexibility

Consistency in rewarding good behavior and punishing bad behavior is a decisive aspect of parenting a child with ADHD. You should keep in mind that your child has a hard time adapting to change compared to their peers. Being too strict will only lead to further frustration and disappointment.

Allow your child to make mistakes because they're essential to the learning process. In addition, if they display unusual behavior that isn't harmful to others but is just a quirk or a personality characteristic, you shouldn't discourage that behavior. Rather, accept it as part of your child's individuality. Otherwise, you will be inhibiting their ability for self-expression.

Break Tasks Down

When your child is working on a task, they are more likely to abandon it if it's too complex. If the answer is not apparent from the get-go, they might feel frustrated and discouraged because they're unable to stay focused. The best course of action is for you to break tasks down into more manageable pieces. You could use a color-coding system for chores and school assignments that compartmentalizes the different things they have to work on as well as the timeframe they're expected to complete those tasks within. This will help you keep your child from feeling overwhelmed and disheartened. You can also do this for morning and nighttime routines, so they're able to take everything one small step at a time.

Encourage Exercise

Children with ADHD often have a lot of energy to burn. Physical activity and exercise can be an outlet for your child to release some of that energy healthily. They're also able to focus their attention on executing different movements and improving motor skills. Burning off that excess energy through exercise can not only promote better concentration and focus in children with ADHD, but also has the potential to boost their brains and improve their sleep patterns. As a parent, you can encourage physical activity by providing your child with active accessories, like balls, jump ropes, and hula hoops, etc. You can also teach them how to ride a bike or enroll them in an organized sport.

Children are a lot more likely to develop and maintain exercise habits and regimens if the parents are good role models in that regard. Going on hikes or playing outdoors together is a great opportunity for your child to expend their excess energy while building healthy habits that will serve them for a lifetime. Find an activity that is best suited to your child's strengths and that you know they will be able to enjoy.

Spend Some Time in Nature

Research shows that spending time in nature can greatly benefit children with ADHD. The severity of their symptoms significantly decreases the more "green time" they're allocated. Playing in a park surrounded by grass, trees, verdant foliage, and an open sky can soothe your child and give you a much-needed break from the daily routine. Joining your child in a park or a natural setting is an amazing opportunity for you to get a breath of fresh air as well.

Keep Your Child Busy

Idle time can further exacerbate your child's symptoms. When they don't have any tasks to complete, chores to do, or activities to keep them entertained, your child takes that opportunity to unleash their hyperactivity and create chaos. So, you must keep your child busy to fill up their time. However, you don't want to exhaust them with a pile of things to do because they will feel overwhelmed and unable to cope with the impossible number of assignments you're giving them. Enroll your child in extracurricular activities, like sports, art classes, or music practice. While at home, you can organize a schedule that includes simple activities to keep them busy, things like playing games with their siblings, coloring, drawing, or helping you in the kitchen. Try not to make video games and screen time your go-to time filler, because based on the nature of the content they're exposed to, that can sometimes accentuate your child's symptoms.

Promote Good Sleep Hygiene

Sleep deprivation is often the cause of a lack of focus and difficulty concentrating. In a child with ADHD, insufficient sleep can be even more detrimental than that. Your child needs as much sleep as their peers if not more, but they probably tend to get less than adequate sleep. This is mainly due to their distractibility and hyperactivity; because of their symptoms, their brains are overstimulated, so they have trouble falling asleep on time.

A structured and consistent bedtime is the best strategy you can use to remedy this issue. Help your child practice good sleep hygiene by decreasing their screen time, especially in the hours leading to their bedtime. Opt for calming and relaxing activities they can do an hour or so before bed, like reading or coloring. You can also make the environment more tranquil and peaceful by dimming the lights, using appeasing aromas like lavender, making their bed as comfortable as possible, and minimizing background noises. If they still find it hard to fall asleep, you can use soothing music accompanied by the sounds of nature or you can create white noise with radio static or the buzzing of an electric fan.

Practice Healthy Eating

While dietary regimens may not have direct effects on your child's ADHD, food does affect their mental state and by extension their behavior. Keeping close watch of what your child eats, how much they eat, and when they eat it is important. All children can benefit from a balanced diet and regular mealtimes. This is especially necessary for kids with ADHD because their impulsivity and distractibility can lead to them missing meals or engaging in disordered patterns of eating. Without your parental guidance, your child can forget to eat for hours at a time leading to subsequent binges when they finally pay attention to their hunger. To prevent them from developing these unhealthy eating habits, make sure you prepare nutritious meals and snacks for them to consume following a rigorous schedule.

They need the nutrients to nourish their bodies, but they also need the structure that mealtimes can bring into their days. In addition to that, make sure there is no junk food at home, and no processed food that is too sugary and fatty either. You can reward them every once in a while, with one of their favorite treats, but their eating regimen should be healthy for the most part. Giving them supplements that have the daily required dose of vitamins and minerals is also a great way to ensure their bodies are getting the nutrients they need.

Teach Your Child How to Make Friends

A child that struggles with their ADHD often has a difficult time socializing with others, either because they lack the social skills or because they sometimes talk and act in ways that others may consider to be odd or unusual. Kids with ADHD can have a hard time understanding social cues; they can talk too much at a time and interrupt other people's conversations. These behaviors may come across as aggressive or disrespectful. Furthermore, this emotional immaturity makes them a target for teasing and even bullying. However, ADHD children are smart and creative, and they will eventually pick up on those social cues.

They can build their social skills and assimilate acceptable ways of communication. Sometimes, their quirks and distinguishing characteristics that authority figures, such as parents and teachers, may find frustrating will often appeal to kids their age as they might find them unique or even funny.

Although your child can learn how to get along with others and make friends in their own time, you can further accelerate that process and help them make connections with others by teaching them the basics of social skills and rules. You can help your child gain an affinity for listening and reading people's facial expressions and body language. This will allow for smoother interactions with others, especially in group settings. Speak with them about the challenges they encounter when trying to socialize and push them to adjust their approach and make positive changes in the way they communicate. You can even role-play different social scenarios to help them practice their social skills. Don't forget to make it as fun and engaging as possible so your child does not lose interest.

Explain Rather than Command

As a parent, when you give your child a task, chore, or assignment to complete, they may ask questions or require justifications for doing those tasks. While this can get exasperating pretty quickly, you should give reasons that explain where appropriate. Patience is key, so keep those reasons simple. When you do this, it alleviates some worry and confusion in your child because they can better understand what is asked of them. Explaining the reasons for doing a task is also respectful in a way, and your child will appreciate that respect, particularly if they can sense that they're different from others.

Tackle One Issue at a Time

You cannot remedy every single concern at once. It is important for you to pick your battles and prioritize what situations appear to be the most urgent at that time. Let go of the less critical problems temporarily and start with the ones that require your immediate intervention. You can build your way up from there as you run down the list of concerns and how you intend to tackle each issue.

Cut Yourself Some Slack

Fostering the development of a child with a disorder that involves impulsivity, defiance, and limited self-control is truly one of the most challenging tasks any person will ever have to oversee. So, take the time to acknowledge your hard work and recognize that you are doing the best you can. Moreover, you should understand that you are not a failure if your child misbehaves and that you're not the cause or the reason they are acting that way. Know that you can make a difference through your tenacity and cut yourself some slack every now and then.

Stay Calm

Trying to correct and change a pattern of behavior in your child can be difficult and often overwhelming. Remaining calm in challenging situations allows you to communicate better and problem-solve more efficiently. You won't have much success in doing either if you're in the wrong mental space. In addition to caring for your child's routine and schedule, you should also put in the effort when it comes to yours. Implementing some relaxation techniques here and there can help you maintain your cool and reduce stress in those trying times. You can do this by meditating regularly, practicing yoga, exercising, walking in nature, as well as reducing caffeine and alcohol consumption.

Be Kind to Yourself

It's very easy to fall into the temptation of imagining your life as someone else and how much better that must be, but if you speak to another parent of a child with ADHD, you will find that they are likely feeling the same way and going through the same things. So, at the end of the day, be kind to yourself, practice more gratitude, and try to appreciate the challenges you have overcome. Take pride in everything you have achieved because you have come a long way since you first found out about your child's diagnosis. It's a journey, but it's a worthwhile one, nonetheless.

The Don'ts

In addition to learning what it is that you can do to reduce the severity of your child's symptoms, there is also a list of things you shouldn't do, no matter how tempting they may seem. Below is a list of the don'ts for parenting a child with ADHD.

Don't Allow Your Child's ADHD to Be in Control

While some degree of flexibility is necessary when disciplining your child, their ADHD should not be an excuse for poor behavior. Boundaries are essential if you want to make your home a safe and organized space. So, it's important for your child to learn that there are consequences for their misbehaviors. These consequences should be reinforced appropriately and consistently. If you don't always follow through on the consequences, your child might see this as an encouraging sign to continue with their unruly behavior.

Don't See Other Parents as the Enemy

Being protective of your child, especially when they have a disorder like ADHD, is completely natural. It may even seem like other caregivers don't understand them or care about them as much as you do. This is why good communication is crucial.

Talk to other adults that your child has contact with about their ADHD. Explain their likes and dislikes as well as the systems you have established to respond to their behavior. This can be tremendously helpful for you. Moreover, it can facilitate building a relationship of trust with these other adults, so you're comfortable enough for them to care for your child when you are unable to be there for them.

Don't Use Negative Language

Positive feedback is helpful in building your child's confidence. Children with ADHD can often feel inadequate and disliked because they're constantly reprimanded for doing things the wrong way. Reinforcing this through negative language can be hurtful and result in worsening those disruptive patterns of behavior. While it's impossible to be positive at all times, it is important for you as a parent to find an outlet that allows you to vent and express your frustrations, worries, and concerns without taking them out on your child. This could be a friend, a partner, or a therapist. You can also sign up for an online group or forum that is specifically targeted to offer support to parents of children with ADHD.

Don't Get Overwhelmed and Lash Out

When you're overly stressed, this does not only affect your emotional and mental well-being but also translates into the way you deal with and support your child. An overwhelming amount of work, obligations, and family responsibilities can cause you to lash out. This anger leads to feeling guilty for your outburst, which only results in more frustrations and can break the trust you have built with your child. Remember that their behavior is caused by a disorder, and while it might not be visible on the outside, it is still a disability, and it should be treated that way.

Don't Take Rule-Breaking Personally

Breaking the rules is basically an item in every child's job description. So, it's important that when your child does break the rules, you correct that behavior in an objective way. They're not acting out to specifically disrespect you or question your authority. Don't take every mistake they make personally or as a direct reflection of your parenting. Be respectful and be consistent.

Don't Sweat the Small Stuff

When parenting a child with ADHD, you need to be willing to make compromises every now and then. If your child has accomplished 90% of the tasks they were assigned, consider being flexible on the remaining 10%. It is a learning process, and every little effort they expend is worth celebrating. Remember that even the smallest steps count!

If parents addressed every problem and issue they encounter with their children, every day would be stressful, overwhelming, and incredibly unpleasant for everyone involved. Learning to let the little things go can alleviate stress and help you stay focused on remedying the more important behaviors.

Final Words

No matter if people believe in the prevalence of ADHD in our society or how accurately we can explain it and treat it, many of us live in hiding due to the stigma associated with having ADHD. The purpose of this book was to try to shed a better light on the effects ADHD has on the residents of its closed community and how far some of them have to go to reach the semblance of a normal life.

The phenomenon of ADHD, or any mental disorder for that matter, is still a subject of much debate and blind spots, which begs the need for reformatory actions. People with ADHD aren't the only ones to suffer from scrutiny and/or the lacking acknowledgment of their issues. They are not a burden to society; in many scenarios, they are the ones that carry it.

We've given a lot of practical tips and scientific research. Now, only you can decide what the best method of treatment for your specific symptoms is. Whether you choose to medicate with multiple prescriptions or you decide to only use exercise therapy, that is completely up to you.

There are a few more things that are important to remember for all ADHD patients. You should always keep a journal of your symptoms, mood, diet, and activities. Whether it's a daily journal or you simply write down the basic notes and numbers of the day, recording the small things that could influence your ADHD symptoms is important. It will give you the ability to reflect on the choices you've made to see if any might be causing symptoms to worsen.

Make sure that you are utilizing the free sources around you as well, which are present online and with friends. Talk to others about symptoms, and find someone you can open up to.

Find communities through the biggest social media pages, and don't be afraid to start your own forum, blog, or another way to voice your journey.

Always keep in mind that this is a journey that will take time. Some moments you might feel like you've managed your ADHD, and other times, you might feel as if you haven't made any progress. Be mindful of the obstacles you're sure to face, and don't be too hard on yourself on the days that might be more challenging. Don't compare yourself to others, and remember that focusing on what works best for you is the most important aspect of this entire journey.

www.ingramcontent.com/pod-product-compliance
Lightning Source LLC
LaVergne TN
LVHW021735060526
838200LV00052B/3295